OUR SOLAR SYSTEM- PLANETS AND EXOPLANETS VOLUME- 1.2

VINIT YADAV

Copyright © Vinit Yadav
All Rights Reserved.

This book has been published with all efforts taken to make the material error-free after the consent of the author. However, the author and the publisher do not assume and hereby disclaim any liability to any party for any loss, damage, or disruption caused by errors or omissions, whether such errors or omissions result from negligence, accident, or any other cause.

While every effort has been made to avoid any mistake or omission, this publication is being sold on the condition and understanding that neither the author nor the publishers or printers would be liable in any manner to any person by reason of any mistake or omission in this publication or for any action taken or omitted to be taken or advice rendered or accepted on the basis of this work. For any defect in printing or binding the publishers will be liable only to replace the defective copy by another copy of this work then available.

This book is dedicated to respected Astronomer **Anil Kumar Das**. Most of his scientific contributions were in the field of solar physics mainly as an experimenter in the spectrophotometric study of sunspots and the chromosphere. He contributed significantly to the development of the equipment present at the Kodaikanal Observatory and to the growth of numerous young researchers.

Contents

Author

The Author of this book- Our Solar system- Planets and exoplanets are Vinit Yadav. Born in a lower-middle-class family in a small village of Haryana. He is 15 years old while writing this book for astronomy lovers. He always wanted to share his knowledge of Astronomy with others.

This is his first book written towards Astronomy, and his second in life. And will share more knowledge with others through his books!

Hope you will get to learn something knowledgeable in this book.

Preface

Abstract In this Volume-1.2, It is the research and its data carried about The Jovian Planets, Atmosphere and Interiors. Starting from Jupitor, Saturn, Uranus and Neptune Its Interior, Overview, Atmosphere, Axis of Rotation, its magnetic field, Structure, their Moons, Rings about their Missions carried out till now.

Further it is about Planets present in our solar system (Two kind of planets)- Terrestrial and Jovian Planets, Data related to them and their structure.

Exoplanets- In this volume we have also discussed about Exoplanets(their search history, missions etc) in brief.

This Volume is the last of this research paper - Our Solar System-Planets and Exoplanets

CHAPTER ONE

Jovian Planets

The Jovian planets

The outermost planets in our solar system are Jupiter, Saturn, Uranus, and Neptune. They are often called the "Jovian planets," meaning they are like Jupiter. In fact, they are each individual with separate personalities. compares the four outer worlds to each other and to Earth. One striking feature is their size. Jupiter is the largest of the Jovian worlds, over 11 times the diameter of Earth. Saturn is slightly smaller, and Uranus and Neptune are quite a bit smaller than Jupiter and Saturn, but still four times the size of Earth. Pluto, not pictured in the figure, is smaller than Earth's moon but was considered a planet from the time of its discovery in 1930 until a decision by the International Astronomical Union (**IAU**) in 2006 that reclassified Pluto as a dwarf planet. Saturn's rings- They are bright and beautiful and composed of billions of ice particles. Jupiter, Uranus, and Neptune also have rings, but they are not easily detected from Earth.

Atmospheres and Interiors

The four Jovian worlds have hydrogen-rich atmospheres filled with clouds. On Jupiter and Saturn, you can see that the clouds form stripes and bands that circle each planet. You will find traces of these same types of features on Uranus and Neptune, but less distinct.

Models based on observations indicate that the atmospheres of the Jovian planets are not very deep; for example, Jupiter's atmosphere makes up only about one percent of its radius. Below their atmospheres Jupiter and Saturn are mostly liquid, so the old-fashioned term for these planets, gas giants, should probably be changed to liquid giants. Uranus and Neptune are sometimes called ice giants because they contain abundant water in solid forms. Only near their centers do the Jovian planets have cores of dense material with the composition of rock and metal. None of the Jovian worlds has a definite solid surface.

Satellite Systems

We can't really land your spaceship on the Jovian worlds, but you might be able to land on one of their moons. All of the Jovian worlds have extensive satellite systems. In many cases, the moons interact gravitationally, mutually adjusting their orbits and also affecting the planetary ring systems. Some of the moons are geologically active now, while others show signs of past activity.

Jupiter

Jupiter is the largest and most massive of the Jovian planets, containing 71 percent of all the planetary matter in the entire solar system.

The Interior

Although Jupiter is very large, it is only 1.3 times denser than water. For comparison, Earth is more than 5.5 times denser than water. The density of a planet is an important clue about the average composition of the planet's interior. Jupiter's shape also gives information about its interior. Jupiter and the other Jovian planets are all slightly flattened. A world with a large rocky core and mantle would not be flattened much by rotation, but an all-liquid planet would flatten significantly. Thus Jupiter's oblateness, the fraction by which its equatorial diameter exceeds its polar diameter, combined with its average density, helps astronomers calculate what its insides are like.

The interior of Jupiter is mostly liquid hydrogen. The base of the atmosphere is so hot and the pressure is so high that there is no sudden boundary between liquid and gas. Deeper and deeper through the atmosphere, you would find the gas density increasing around you until you were sinking through a liquid, but you would never splash into a distinct liquid surface.

Under very high pressure, liquid hydrogen becomes liquid metallic hydrogen — a material that is a very good conductor of electricity. Model calculations indicate that most of Jupiter's interior is composed of this material. That large mass of conducting liquid, stirred by convection currents and spun by the planet's rapid rotation, drives the dynamo effect and generates a powerful magnetic field. Jupiter's field is over ten times stronger than Earth's.

A planet's magnetic field deflects the solar wind and dominates a volume of space around the planet called the magnetosphere. Jupiter's magnetosphere is 100 times larger than Earth's. If you could see it in the sky, it would be six times larger than the full moon. Just as in the case of Earth, interactions between Jupiter's magnetic field and the solar wind generate powerful electric currents that flow around the planet's magnetic poles. These are visible at ultraviolet wavelengths as rings of auroral lights that are larger in diameter than Earth.

The strong magnetic field around Jupiter traps charged particles from the solar wind in radiation belts a billion times more intense than the Van Allen belts that surround Earth. The spacecraft that have flown through these regions received over 4000 times the radiation that would have been lethal for a human.

At Jupiter's center, a so-called rocky core contains heavier elements, such as iron, nickel, silicon, and so on. With a temperature four times hotter than the surface of the sun and a pressure 50 million times Earth's sea level atmospheric pressure, this material is unlike any rock on Earth. The term rocky core refers to the chemical composition, not to the properties of the material.

Jupiter's Overview

Northern hemisphere

Until 2003, Jupiter's north polar regions hid a secret—a dark spot twice the size of the planet's best-known feature, the Great Red Spot. The dark spot, which is visible only intermittently, appears to be in the highest layers of Jupiter's atmosphere.

Tilt

Jupiter orbits with almost no tilt on its axis, so it has no seasons, and the equator always receives much more heat from solar radiation than the poles. This may contribute to the planet's remarkably stable large-scale weather systems.

Southern hemisphere

Both of Jupiter's poles are partly obscured by a haze, caused by radiation making chemical changes in atmospheric gases. Enormous electrical energy at the poles creates aurorae thousands of times more extensive than those seen in polar latitudes on Earth.

1. The North Temperate Belt has a strong jet stream blowing in the same direction as Jupiter's rotation.
2. The Great Red Spot is a giant storm that sits between the South Equatorial Belt and the South Tropical Zone.
3. The South Tropical Zone is Jupiter's most active weather region, with a strong jet stream moving in the opposite direction of the planet's rotation.

4. Complex, ribbon-like features called festoons form in the turbulent boundaries between belts and zones.
5. The Equatorial Zone is a belt of bright, high-altitude clouds.
6. The South Equatorial Belt is usually the broadest and darkest cloud band on the planet.
7. **Atmosphere Jupiter's** atmosphere, mostly hydrogen gas with some helium, extends upward for more than 3,100 miles (5,000 km) to merge with interplanetary space.

Jupiter's Complex Atmosphere

It is a Common Misconception that Jupiter is a ball of gases. In fact, as you have just learned, Jupiter is almost entirely a liquid planet. Its atmosphere is only a thin outer skin of turbulent gases and clouds.

1. The atmosphere is hydrogen-rich, and the clouds are confined to a shallow layer.
2. The positions of the cloud layers are at certain temperatures within the atmosphere where ammonia (NH_3), ammonium hydrosulfide (NH_4SH), and water (H_2O) can condense.
3. The pattern of colored cloud bands circling the planet like stripes on a child's ball is called belt–zone circulation. This pattern is related to the high- and low-pressure areas found in Earth's atmosphere.
4. The large circular or oval spots seen in Jupiter's clouds are circulating storms that can remain stable for decades or even centuries.

1). Humans will probably never visit Jupiter's atmosphere. Its cloud layers are deathly cold, and the deeper layers that are warmer have crushingly high pressure. There is no free oxygen to breathe; the gases are roughly three-quarters hydrogen and quarter helium, plus small amounts of water vapor, methane, ammonia, and similar molecules. Traces of sulfur and molecules containing sulfur probably make it smell bad. Of course, Jupiter has no surface, so there isn't even a place to stand. Jupiter is a nice planet to look at, but it's not a place to visit.

1a). 1 Human will probably never visit Jupiter's atmosphere. Its cloud layers are deathly cold, and the deeper layers that are warmer have crushingly high pressure. There is no free oxygen to breathe; the gases are roughly three-quarters hydrogen and quarter helium, plus small amounts of water vapor, methane, ammonia, and similar molecules. Traces of sulfur and molecules containing sulfur probably make it smell bad. Of course, Jupiter has no surface, so there isn't even a place to stand. Jupiter is a nice planet to look at, but it's not a place to visit. The only spacecraft to enter Jupiter's atmosphere was the Galileo probe. Released from the Galileo spacecraft, the probe entered Jupiter's atmosphere in December 1995. It parachuted through the upper atmosphere of clear hydrogen, released its heat shield, and then fell through Jupiter's stormy atmosphere until it was crushed by the increasing pressure.

° Jupiter's atmosphere is a very thin layer of turbulent gas above the liquid interior. It makes up only about 1 percent of the radius of the planet.

° The Great Red Spot at right is a giant circulating storm in one of the southern zones. It has lasted at least 300 years since astronomers first noticed it after the invention of the telescope. Smaller spots are also circulating storms.

2). The visible clouds on Jupiter are composed of ammonia crystals, but models predict that deeper layers of clouds contain ammonia hydrosulfide crystals, and deeper still lies a cloud layer of water droplets. These compounds are normally white, so planetary scientists think the colors arise from small amounts of other molecules formed in reactions powered by lightning or sunlight.

3). On Earth, the temperature difference between the poles and equator drives a wave-shaped high-speed wind that organizes the high- and low-pressure areas into cyclonic circulations familiar from weather maps.

The poles and equator on Jupiter are about the same temperature, perhaps because of heat rising from the interior. Consequently, there are no wave-shaped winds, and the planet's rapid rotation stretches the high- and low-pressure areas into belts and zones that circle the planet.

On both Earth and Jupiter, winds circulate clockwise around the high-pressure areas in the northern hemisphere and counter-clockwise south of the equator.

JUPITER STRUCTURE

GIGANTIC THOUGH JUPITER IS, THE MATERIALS THAT FORM THE PLANET ARE COMPARATIVELY LIGHT. DESPITE THIS, FORCES OF GRAVITATIONAL CONTRACTION DEEP INSIDE JUPITER TURN THE PLANET'S INTERIOR INTO A POWERHOUSE OF ENERGY.

While Jupiter's interior is almost entirely pure hydrogen, the planet's upper layers are enriched with more complex gases that form the well-defined striped atmosphere. Around 600 miles (1,000 km) below this apparent "surface," pressures are high enough to transform hydrogen gas into a liquid. Some 12,500 miles (20,000 km) farther inward, pressure is so intense—many millions of times the atmospheric pressure on Earth—that it tears the hydrogen atoms apart, freeing their hold over electrons and causing the hydrogen to behave like liquid metal.

Within the planet, denser materials sink downward, while the lighter materials rise up. The power this generates allows Jupiter to pump out more energy than it receives from the Sun, mostly in the form of heat and radio waves. Huge electrical currents in the metallic hydrogen layer create the most powerful magnetic field of any planet in the solar system.

1. Core

The existence of a solid core at Jupiter's heart is unproven but likely. It could be the original seed around which the planet coalesced, or possibly a growing nucleus formed by Jupiter's ongoing contraction

1. Liquid metallic

hydrogen layer Liquid hydrogen atoms break down under heat and pressure to create a layer of liquid metallic hydrogen. This fluid, produced under extreme conditions, never occurs naturally on Earth

3. Liquid layer

Below Jupiter's cloud layer, increasing pressure gradually causes the planet's hydrogen to act like a liquid rather than a gas.

Temperatures at the center may be higher than 36,000°F (20,000°C), which is hotter than the surface of the Sun.

Swirling currents within the liquid metallic hydrogen layer generate a gigantic magnetic field around Jupiter.

Jupiter's upper layers contain a chemical cocktail that includes ammonia, methane, water, and hydrogen sulfide.

Jupiter's layers This model shows Jupiter's internal structure divided into sharply defined layers. However, the transformation of hydrogen from gas to liquid in the depths of the planet is gradual and no obvious meeting point marks the boundary between the phases.

Saturn

Saturn is most famous for its beautiful rings, easily visible through the telescopes of modern amateur astronomers. Large Earth-based telescopes have explored the planet for many decades. The first close-up views came when two Voyager probes flew past Saturn in 1980 and 1981. The Cassini spacecraft went into orbit around Saturn in 2004 and began an extended exploration of the planet, its rings, and its moons.

All the giant planets have ring systems, but Saturn is the glory of the solar system. These concentric disk-like platters are composed of countless ringlets, each of which consists of millions of orbiting ice fragments of varying size and composition.

Fact- Saturn's density is less than water—placed in a large enough ocean, the planet would float.

Northern hemisphere

Saturn's north polar region is remarkable for a long-lived hexagonal cloud structure, more than 17,000 miles (27,000 km) across, with a huge storm at its center. This weather system, which is different from any other so far seen in the solar system, is thought to be caused by a circumpolar jet stream.

Tilted axis

Saturn's axis of rotation is tilted at an angle of 26.7°, so we view the planet and its rings at different angles throughout its 29.5-Earth-year orbit, as either the north or south pole tips toward the Sun. When the rings lie edge-on, they are invisible to observers on Earth.

Southern hemisphere

The south polar region of Saturn is dominated by a hurricane-like storm almost the diameter of Earth and rotating about 340 mph (550 km/h) faster than the planet itself. The eye of the storm is ringed by clouds up to 45 miles (75 km) high.

Rings and bands

Like Jupiter, Saturn has a distinctive banded appearance, although with much paler colors. The enormous ring system extends far beyond the planet; its main elements have a total diameter of over 170,000 miles (270,000 km).

SATURN STRUCTURE

SATURN IS SIMILAR IN COMPOSITION AND STRUCTURE TO JUPITER, BUT IT IS CONSIDERABLY LESS MASSIVE THAN ITS

NEIGHBOR. ITS WEAKER GRAVITY ALLOWS ITS LAYERS TO EXPAND OUTWARD, LOWERING ITS OVERALL DENSITY.

Saturn's low density and its greater distance from the Sun combine to make its outer layers significantly cooler than those of Jupiter—a feature that is most evident in the formation of ammonia-ice clouds across the entire upper atmosphere. These yellowish-white clouds give Saturn its color. Beneath the visible cloud layers, Saturn is roughly 96 percent hydrogen, 3 percent helium, and 1 percent other, heavier elements that concentrate at the center. As with Jupiter, the gradual sorting of elements by density drives a "heat engine" that allows Saturn to pump out 2.5 times more energy than it receives from the Sun.

Core

Saturn's core has a diameter of around 15,500 miles (25,000 km). Heated to more than 22,000°F (11,700°C), it may be a molten mix of rock and metal rather than a solid body, and may have 9–22 times the mass of Earth.

Liquid metallic

hydrogen At a depth of around 9,300 miles (15,000 km), hydrogen molecules begin to break down into individual atoms, creating a sea of electrically conducting liquid metal with currents that generate Saturn's powerful magnetic field.

Liquid hydrogen

Molecular hydrogen (H_2) condenses into liquid form gradually with increasing depth. Liquid hydrogen becomes dominant below about 600 miles (1,000 km).

Atmosphere

Saturn's outermost layer is about 600 miles (1,000 km) deep and is dominated by hydrogen gas. Clouds in this region form from the condensation of different chemical compounds, including ammonia and water.

Complex atmosphere

Saturn's placid appearance belies its dynamic interior and stormy atmosphere. Enhanced color images from spacecraft have revealed the presence of turbulent cloud layers beneath the outer ammonia haze. These cloud layers are dominated by ammonium hydrogen sulfide at high altitudes and by water ice at lower levels.

SATURN'S RINGS

SATURN IS ENCIRCLED BY THE MOST SPECTACULAR RING SYSTEM IN THE SOLAR SYSTEM. THE BRIGHT PLATTERS VISIBLE FROM

EARTH CONSIST ALMOST ENTIRELY OF ICE FRAGMENTS THAT WHIRL AROUND THE PLANET IN CONCENTRIC RINGLETS.

Saturn's rings contain billions of pieces of ice, varying from house-sized boulders to minute crystals. Jostling together, these particles are constrained by the planet's gravity to orbit in a flat plane above Saturn's equator. The system is complex, with each large ring being made up of many narrow ringlets. Several distinct gaps between the rings are created by the gravitational pull of Saturn's more distant moons and the clumping together of material within the rings themselves. The particles consist predominantly of water ice, which makes them naturally reflective. Although their surfaces become dust-coated over time, constant collisions within the rings cause them to fracture, exposing bright new facets.

Fact- In places, Saturn's main rings are a mere 10 yards (10 m) thick.

Rings within rings

Astronomers have identified at least nine major rings. The A and B rings are the brightest and contain the largest ice particles; white and purple denote particles larger than 2 in (5 cm) in this false-color image. A wide gap called the Cassini division separates the A and B rings. The paler C and D rings extend inward from the B ring and contain particles less than 2 in (5 cm) in size (here, colored green and blue).

Outer rings

Beyond Saturn's familiar main rings are several hazier, darker, and much less sharply defined outer rings. These tenuous haloes of dust and ice become visible only with the use of special imaging techniques. Below, a backlit view of Saturn, with the Sun obscured by the planet's disk, reveals the faint E ring. This cloud of microscopic particles is fed by the plumes of ice that erupt from the surface of Enceladus, one of Saturn's most interesting moons. Unlike the slim main rings, the E ring is more than 1,250 miles (2,000 km) thick.

The Phoebe ring

In 2009, astronomers using NASA's infrared Spitzer Space Telescope discovered a vast ring of dust thought to be produced by meteor impacts on one of Saturn's outer moons, Phoebe. Tilted at 27 degrees to the other rings, the Phoebe ring begins at around 2.5 million miles (4 million km) from Saturn and extends outward for more than three times that distance.

The main rings lie within Saturn's Roche lobe—a region where the planet's gravity prevents them from coalescing into a single moon.

MISSIONS TO SATURN

SATURN AND ITS MOONS HAVE BEEN VISITED BY SEVERAL SPACECRAFT SINCE THE 1970S. THE FIRST MISSIONS WERE FLYBYS, BUT MORE RECENTLY A DECADE-LONG INVESTIGATION WAS UNDERTAKEN BY NASA'S CASSINI ORBITER.

Saturn was a key destination for the Pioneer missions that paved the way for the exploration of the outer solar system. While Pioneer 10 merely flew past Jupiter, Pioneer 11 used a gravitational slingshot from the giant planet to propel itself to Saturn in September 1979. The twin Voyager probes arrived in November 1980 and August 1981 and gave the first detailed views of Saturn's intriguing family of moons. Saturn was not revisited until 2004, when Cassini (and its companion, the Huygens Titan probe) became the first craft to orbit the ringed planet.

Voyager spacecraft The two identical Voyager spacecraft each weighed around 1,700 lb (773 kg) and carried 231 lb (105 kg) of scientific instruments. A large radio dish (high-gain antenna) kept the craft in touch with Earth, while a radioactive power source generated electricity without the need for solar panels. Each mission carried with it a Voyager Golden Record—a gold disc inscribed with information about Earth.

Discoveries The Voyager flybys confirmed the existence of countless individual ringlets within Saturn's main rings, as well as short-lived structures such as radial spokes. Although Titan's thick atmosphere proved impenetrable, the Voyagers discovered surface features on several of the other moons for the first time, as well as details of Saturn's own weather systems.

Cassini

The enormous Cassini spacecraft is the size of a bus and has a mass of 4,740 lb (2,150 kg), making it the largest and most complex interplanetary craft sent into space so far. Onboard instruments include advanced radar, visible and infrared mapping cameras, magnetometers, and particle analysis tools. Cassini also transported the Huygens Titan probe, adding a further 770 lb (350 kg) to the overall payload.

Launch In October 1997, Cassini blasted off from Cape Canaveral aboard a Titan-IVB/Centaur rocket. Its complex trajectory— including two flybys of Venus, one of Earth, and one of Jupiter, gaining speed with each encounter— meant that Cassini took nearly seven years to reach Saturn.

URANUS

ENIGMATIC URANUS KEEPS ITS SECRETS HIDDEN UNDER AN ALMOST CLOUDLESS FACE. UNIQUELY, URANUS SPINS ON ITS SIDE AS

IT ORBITS THE SUN. ALTHOUGH NOT THE FARTHEST PLANET FROM THE SUN, IT IS THE COLDEST OF ALL.

Uranus is only one-third the diameter of Jupiter and only one-twentieth as massive. Four times farther from the sun than Jupiter, its atmosphere is almost 100°C colder than Jupiter's.

Uranus never grew massive enough to capture large amounts of gas from the nebula as Jupiter and Saturn did, so it has much less hydrogen and helium. Its internal pressure is enough less than Jupiter's that it should not contain any liquid metallic hydrogen. Models of Uranus based in part on its density and oblateness suggest that it has a small core of heavy elements and a deep mantle of partly solid water. Although that material is referred to as ice, it would not be anything like ice on Earth at the temperatures and pressures inside Uranus. The mantle also probably contains rocky material plus dissolved ammonia and methane. Circulation in that electrically conducting mantle may generate the planet's peculiar magnetic fi eld, which is highly inclined to its axis of rotation. Above the mantle lies a deep hydrogen and helium atmosphere.

Uranus rotates on its side, with its equator inclined 98° to its orbit.

As a result the winter–summer contrast is extreme, with the sun passing near each of the planet's celestial poles at the solstices, so half of the planet is in perpetual darkness and the other half in perpetual light for the 21 year–long summer and winter seasons.

Northern hemisphere

Night and day at the poles each last for 42 years. The northern polar region is now coming into sight, brightening as Uranus moves around the Sun; the planet's changing seasons expose the region to more intense sunlight.

Tilt

Uranus's axis is tilted at almost a right angle to its orbit, and the planet rotates the opposite way to all the other planets except Venus. This is probably because Uranus was "knocked over" by a giant impact soon after the planet's formation.

Southern hemisphere

Voyager 2 sped directly toward the south pole of the tipped-up planet, which at the time was midway through its 42-year day. When the images of Uranus were enhanced, this was the brightest region; it is now fading.

During Uranus's northern summer, the northern atmosphere becomes more active as it warms up.

Lacking methane clouds, the region around the equator is darker.

Ice giant

Uranus is a giant planet four times wider than Earth. Its density indicates that Uranus consists mainly of water, ammonia, and methane—substances that are normally frozen at such a vast distance from the Sun.

URANUS STRUCTURE

BENEATH AN ATMOSPHERE TINGED BLUE-GREEN BY METHANE LIES A HUGE, SLUSHY OCEAN SURROUNDING A CORE OF HOT ROCK. THE PLANET'S LOPSIDED MAGNETIC FIELD MAY BE GENERATED BY A LAYER OF ELECTRICALLY CHARGED WATER.

In the depths of Uranus's hidden ocean, water molecules break down to form a soup of hydrogen and oxygen ions. Currents in this sea of electrically charged particles are thought to generate Uranus's magnetic field, which is lopsided and off-center.

Unlike the other giant planets, Uranus radiates less heat into space than it receives from the Sun. This may be because it was suddenly cooled by the immense impact that knocked the infant planet on its side.

Other planets spin like tops—Uranus rolls like a marble.

Core

Uranus's core is slightly less massive than planet Earth. A molten mixture of iron and magma, it has a temperature of more than 9,000°F (5,000°C) and is squeezed by pressure 10 million times greater than atmospheric pressure on Earth's surface.

Mantle

Astronomers call Uranus an ice giant because water, ammonia, and methane— the planet's main constituents—are normally frozen this far from the Sun. However, the high temperatures on the planet melt these substances to form a slushy ocean with a depth of 9,300 miles (15,000 km).

Atmosphere

The "air" on Uranus is mainly hydrogen and helium. There are layers of clouds at different depths in the atmosphere. Unique among the giant planets, Uranus has a tenuous outer atmosphere that is several times larger than the planet itself.

At the base of the mantle is a layer of superionic water—electrically charged hydrogen and oxygen—that glows yellow.

Clouds of ammonia form in the atmosphere. The deepest clouds consist of frozen water droplets.

The brightest and densest ring, Epsilon, is shepherded by two tiny moons, Cordelia and Ophelia, whose gravity helps maintain its shape.

Rings

Uranus has a set of 13 rings. The first rings were discovered in 1977 when they unexpectedly blocked out the light of a distant star. Other rings were detected by Voyager 2 in 1986 and by the Hubble Space Telescope in 2003–05. All the rings of Uranus are narrow and, unlike Saturn's brilliant rings, as dark as coal.

ASTRONOMERS DIVIDE URANUS'S 27 MOONS INTO THREE GROUPS: FIVE MAJOR MOONS, 13 SMALL INNER MOONS, AND NINE SMALL OUTER MOONS.

Inner moons

The five largest moons, which orbit directly above the planet's tipped-up equator, were formed from the same spinning disk of gas and ice as Uranus itself. The 13 moons that lie closer to Uranus are in unstable orbits: past collisions have filled this region with rubble that still orbits Uranus, now corralled into narrow rings by the gravity of nearby moons.

Umbriel

The darkest of Uranus's moons, Umbriel is composed mainly of ice, coated in a layer of dark material perhaps made of organic (carbon-rich) compounds.

Oberon

This is the outermost of Uranus's five major moons. It is a mixture of ice and rock, and its dark surface has a reddish tinge. Debris from space has smashed into Oberon, making it the most cratered of all Uranus's moons; one crater's central peak is 36,000 ft (11,000 m) high—taller than Mount Everest.

Diagram, engineering drawing Description automatically generated

Titania

Titania is Uranus's largest moon and the eighth-biggest moon in the solar system. Titania's face is blemished by massive canyons and scarps, which formed when this moon expanded soon after its formation. Titania may have a very tenuous atmosphere of carbon dioxide.

Outer moons

The nine outer moons are small icy worlds— Kuiper belt objects or the nuclei of comets— that have been captured by Uranus's gravity. The largest, Sycorax, is only 93 miles (150 km) across, while diminutive Trinculo has a diameter of fewer than 12 miles (20 km). These moons follow strange orbits, tilted at odd angles and looping in and out; Margaret has the highest eccentricity (least circular orbit) of any moon in the solar system.

NEPTUNE

Planet Neptune is Almost exactly the same size as Uranus, Neptune has a similar interior. Model calculations predict that a small core of heavy elements lies within a slushy mantle of water, ices, and rocky materials below a hydrogen-rich atmosphere. Yet, Neptune looks quite different on the outside from Uranus; Neptune is dramatically blue and has active cloud formations. Neptune's dark blue tint is caused by its atmospheric composition of one and a half times more methane than Uranus. Methane absorbs red photons better than blue and scatters blue photons better than red, giving Neptune a blue color and Uranus a green-blue color.

Atmospheric circulation on Neptune is much more dramatic than on Uranus. When Voyager 2 flew by Neptune in 1989, the largest feature was the Great Dark Spot. Roughly the size of Earth, the spot seemed to be an atmospheric circulation pattern much like Jupiter's Great Red Spot. Smaller spots were visible in Neptune's atmosphere, and photos showed they were circulating like hurricanes. More recently, the Hubble Space Telescope has photographed Neptune and found that the Great Dark Spot is gone and new cloud formations have appeared. Evidently, the weather on Neptune is changeable.

The atmospheric activity on Neptune is apparently driven by heat flowing from the interior plus some contribution by dim sunlight 30 AU from the sun. The heat causes convection in the atmosphere, which the rapid rotation of the planet converts into high-speed winds, high-level white clouds of methane ice crystals, and rotating storms visible as spots. Neptune may have more activity than Uranus because it has more heat flowing out of its interior, for reasons that are unclear.

Tilt Neptune's axis is tilted at a similar angle to Earth's, so like Earth, the planet experiences seasons as it moves around the Sun. However, Neptune is so far from the Sun that each of its seasons lasts for more than 40 years.

Northern hemisphere

It is currently winter in Neptune's northern hemisphere, so there is little activity in the region. Voyager 2 flew less than 3,000 miles (5,000 km) above the northern hemisphere's cloud tops—the closest of all its planetary encounters.

Cirrus clouds—wispy streamers of frozen methane—float at an altitude of 30 miles (50 km).

Blue planet

When Voyager 2 arrived at Neptune, it found a blue planet with prominent weather systems, orbited by a large, rocky moon. While Earth's blue color comes from its oceans, Neptune's azure hue is caused by its deep methane atmosphere.

NEPTUNE STRUCTURE

Neptune is the third most massive planet, after Jupiter and Saturn. It is slightly smaller than neighboring Uranus because it has a thinner atmosphere, but its deeper liquid mantle makes it more massive overall. Like Uranus, Neptune is sometimes called an ice giant because it formed from volatile compounds that existed as ices in the early solar system—mainly water, ammonia, and methane. Inside the planet's hot, dense interior, however, these compounds exist in a liquid form today.

Neptune's interior generates vast amounts of heat; around 60 percent more warmth wells up from deep inside the planet than arrives at its surface from the Sun. The heat and pressure in the lower mantle are so intense that methane may split into its constituent elements carbon and hydrogen, creating an ocean of liquid diamond around the core

Core

Neptune's core weighs 20 percent more than Earth's and, like our planet, consists of rock and iron. Relative to Neptune's size, it's the most massive core of the giant planets. The core's central temperature probably exceeds 9,000°F (5,000°C).

Mantle

Most of Neptune's mass is in its mantle—a deep ocean of water, ammonia, and methane. Toward the bottom of the mantle, water molecules break up into oxygen and hydrogen ions. These electrically charged particles may be responsible for generating Neptune's magnetic field, which is tilted relative to the planet's axis of rotation.

Atmosphere

The turbulent cloud patterns in Neptune's atmosphere are only skin-deep, and the planet's dark-spot weather systems are short-lived. The deeper atmosphere extends one-fifth of the way to the core. It consists mainly of hydrogen and helium, with traces of methane providing a blue color.

Ring system

Neptune has five very faint rings. Three are narrow, like the rings of Uranus, but two are broader bands of dust. The ring system was first detected from Earth during the 1980s when it was noticed that something was blocking the light of the stars behind Neptune.

Galle is the innermost of Neptune's five rings. The existence of Neptune's rings was confirmed by the visit of Voyager 2 in 1989.

Le Verrier ring is shepherded by the tiny moon Despina; the moon's gravity helps to keep material within the ring.

Adams ring, the outermost of Neptune's rings, is unique in the solar system: its brightest regions are five distinct arcs following the same orbital path but separated from each other.

Clouds of ammonia and water condense in the atmosphere.

THE NEPTUNE SYSTEM

LIKE ALL THE GAS GIANTS IN THE OUTER SOLAR SYSTEM, NEPTUNE IS SURROUNDED BY A FASCINATING, DYNAMIC ENVIRONMENT. HOST TO AT LEAST 14 MOONS, THE PLANET IS ALSO CIRCLED BY A SET OF FIVE VERY THIN RINGS.

The first moon to be identified was mighty Triton—only 17 days after Neptune itself was discovered in 1846. The astronomer who tracked it down was Englishman William Lassell. A fortune amassed as a brewer in the northern town of Bolton enabled Lassell to build giant telescopes and indulge his passion for astronomy.

Over a century passed before Nereid was discovered in 1949; a third moon, Larissa, followed in 1981. The rest of the moons were found more recently, either by the Voyager 2 spacecraft, which flew past Neptune in 1989 or by powerful, ground-based telescopes. The latest addition to the family—as yet unnamed—was spotted by the Hubble Space Telescope in 2013. All currently named moons of Neptune are named after water gods and spirits in Greek mythology.

Triton

This moon is an oddball, orbiting its planet backward—a characteristic not shared by any other large moon in the solar system. Like the outer moons, Triton was captured by the planet's gravity. The taming of such a large body wreaked havoc on the Neptune system, sending other moons into strange orbits. Triton's own orbit isn't stable: its destiny is to crash into Neptune.

Outer moons

None of Neptune's outer moons has a circular orbit. Instead, they loop around the planet in great ellipses. Some of the orbits are highly inclined, and these orbits vary between prograde (forward) and retrograde (backward). All the outer moons, bar Nereid, are comparatively tiny. The majority of these moonlets were probably captured from the icy Kuiper belt by Neptune's gravity.

S/2004 N1

Yet to be officially named, S/2004 N1 measures just 12 miles (20 km) across, making it Neptune's smallest moon. It was found in 2013 when astronomers scrutinized images of the arcs in Adams ring taken by the Hubble Space Telescope between 2004 and 2009. As with all of Neptune's inner moons, the surface of S/2004 N1 is extremely dark.

Thalassa

Discovered by Voyager 2, Thalassa is irregularly shaped—possibly even a disk—and it shares the potential of many of its inner companions to spiral into Neptune.

Despina

Another Voyager 2 find, Despina is the third moon from Neptune. In legend, Despina was a nymph—the daughter of Poseidon and Demeter. Like Galatea, Despina is slowly spiraling into Neptune.

Neptune's innermost ring, Galle orbits about 26,000 miles (42,000 km) from the planet's surface.

Naiad

Named after the legendary Greek Naiads, the nymphs of streams, this is Neptune's closest moon. It hugs the planet just 14,600 miles (23,500 km) above Neptune's cloud tops. The irregularly shaped satellite will eventually collide with Neptune.

The Adams ring is Neptune's outermost ring, nearly 38,500 miles (62,000 km) from the planet and only about 22 miles (35 km) wide.

Galatea

Galatea is a small, irregularly shaped body that shepherds the particles of Neptune's outermost Adams ring. It has an unstable orbit and will either break up to form a new ring or spiral into Neptune.

The dusty Le Verrier ring may be shepherded by the moon, Despina.

The broadest ring in the system, Lassell is about 2,500 miles (4,000 km) across.

The Arago ring forms a slightly brighter outer boundary than the Lassell ring.

Larissa

This moon commemorates a lover of the sea god Poseidon. Larissa is the fourth-largest of Neptune's satellites, at 121 miles (194 km) in diameter. Voyager 2 images reveal Larissa to be heavily cratered. The moon probably assembled itself from clouds of rubble produced by collisions between earlier moons.

Proteus

Proteus is the largest of Neptune's inner moons. Discovered by the Voyager 2 spacecraft in 1989, it is irregular in shape. This moon has been heavily battered by impacts; its largest crater measures 125 miles (200 km) across, and its surface is crisscrossed by a network of valleys and grooves.

Inner moons

In contrast to Neptune's outer moons, the inner moons follow nearly circular orbits around the planet, although some of these orbits are unstable. These moons formed along with Neptune, rather than being captured later. The innermost moons shepherd the material in Neptune's rings, which astronomers suspect is debris from collisions between former inner moons.

CHAPTER TWO

Exoplanets Introduction

EXOPLANETS

In the search for other worlds, the last decades have probably been among the

most exciting over the past centuries, possibly since the years of the Copernican

heliocentrism and the discovery by Galileo of the Moons around Jupiter. The large

series of breakthroughs in the search for exoworlds make this recent period a rather

remarkable time in the history of astronomy which appears to be as fascinating as

the one about 400 years ago when humankind started to abandon geocentrism.

During the past 25 years, we have witnessed the detection of planets orbiting

thousands of nearby and distant stars. Since the discovery of the first planets around

pulsars in the early 1990s and the first Jupiter-mass planet around the solar-type

star 51 Peg in 1995, a large diversity of planetary systems, has been identified in

the nearby universe. Efficient hunting programs have provided increasing statistical

evidence that planets are very common around stars. More than 50% of the stars

in our galaxy may host planetary systems and therefore, tens of billions may await discovery. The detection rate of exoplanets has only increased with time, reaching

values above one exoplanet discovery per day. The number of known exoplanets,

several thousand, will considerably increase in the coming decade thanks to the

many search programs already started or planned for ground and space telescopes.

The study of this extremely rich population of planetary systems will lead to a

better understanding of their architecture and the physics involved in the formation

processes. Ultimately, the ongoing search and characterization work may unveil

planets with adequate conditions to sustain the development of life and will pave

the road to the discovery of exolife.

Planets with masses similar to those existing in the Solar System are frequently

found in other planetary systems, displaying very different physical conditions.

Exoplanets appear in a large range of orbital separations around a variety of stars

and therefore are subject to very different stellar irradiations. The properties of the

planets depend heavily on their mass, chemical composition, stellar irradiation, and

on their interaction with the host stars' gravity, radiation, and magnetic field. Observations

have revealed and will continue bringing to light an enormous diversity of

planets and planetary systems conforming to an exceptional set of laboratories that

will challenge our knowledge of physics, chemistry, geology, and biology.

Evidence for the existence of terrestrial planets is compelling, and planets

with similar mass, size, and physical conditions potentially similar to the Earth have already been discovered. Planet Proxima b in the nearest star to the Sun,

detected using Doppler radial velocity measurements, is the closest example of

a continuously increasing family. Such rocky planets may host liquid water,

and the characterization of their thin atmospheres will be an extraordinary challenge,

even for the new generation of extremely large telescopes. Proxima b is

not known to transit its parent star, and direct imaging and spectroscopy with

coronographs assisted by Adaptive Optics on very large and extremely large

telescopes is a promising way to obtain information on its atmospheric properties.

Identifying tracers of biological activity will possibly require new technological

advances.

The Kepler space observatory and other ground-based observatories have identified

a large number of transiting planets, including those of Earth-size. Series

of radial velocity measurements of the host stars could in principle achieve a

determination of the masses for these small planets, which typically induce radial

velocity semi-amplitudes of tens of cm/s in solar type stars. The advent of a new

generation of ultra-stable high dispersion spectrographs at very large telescopes

(ESPRESSO is the first to achieve 10 cm/s) will make possible such measurements

in a fraction of the detected systems, leading to the obtainment of planet densities

and further insight on the formation processes of terrestrial planets. In multiple

transiting planet systems, transit time variability observations can also provide a

determination of masses.

Bright stars with transiting Earth-size planets offer an excellent opportunity to
study planet atmospheric properties with JWST and the ELTs. A large effort is
currently undertaken to search for transiting planets in the habitable zone of nearby
stars using a series of dedicated ground-based telescopes (MEarth, SPECULOOS,
etc.) and space observatories (TESS). In the future, other space telescopes like
JWST, CHEOPS, and PLATO and the extremely large telescopes (EELT, TMT,
GMT) will bring exceptional capacities for the characterization of the atmospheres
of a large variety of exoplanets, including the new terrestrials.